America
Revealed

America Revealed

Tracing Our History Beneath the Surface and Behind the Scenes

LIFE

Editor
Robert Sullivan

Art Director
Ian Denning

Picture Editor
Barbara Baker Burrows

Senior Editor
Robert Andreas

Associate Picture Editor
Donna F. Aceto

Senior Reporter
Hildegard Anderson

Copy Chief
Pamela Warren

Production Manager
Michael H. Roseman

Picture Researchers
Sarah Burrows,
Joan Shweky

**Time Inc.
Home Entertainment**

President
Rob Gursha

**Vice President, Branded
Businesses**
David Arfine

**Executive Director,
Marketing Services**
Carol Pittard

**Director, Retail & Special
Sales**
Tom Mifsud

Director of Finance
Tricia Griffin

Marketing Director
Kenneth Maehlum

Assistant Director
Ann Marie Ross

**Editorial Operations
Manager**
John Calvano

Associate Product Managers
Jennifer Dowell,
Meredith Shelley

Assistant Product Manager
Michelle Kuhr

Special thanks to:
Victoria Alfonso, Suzanne
DeBenedetto, Robert Dente,
Gina Di Meglio, Peter Harper,
Roberta Harris, Natalie McCrea,
Jessica McGrath, Jonathan
Polsky, Emily Rabin, Mary Jane
Rigoroso, Steven Sandonato,
Tara Sheehan, Bozena
Szwagulinski, Marina
Weinstein, Niki Whelan

Dust Bowl America, 1937 (page 120).
Previous pages: The tufa towers at
California's Mono Lake became
visible only after Los Angeles began
to siphon off its water (page 122).

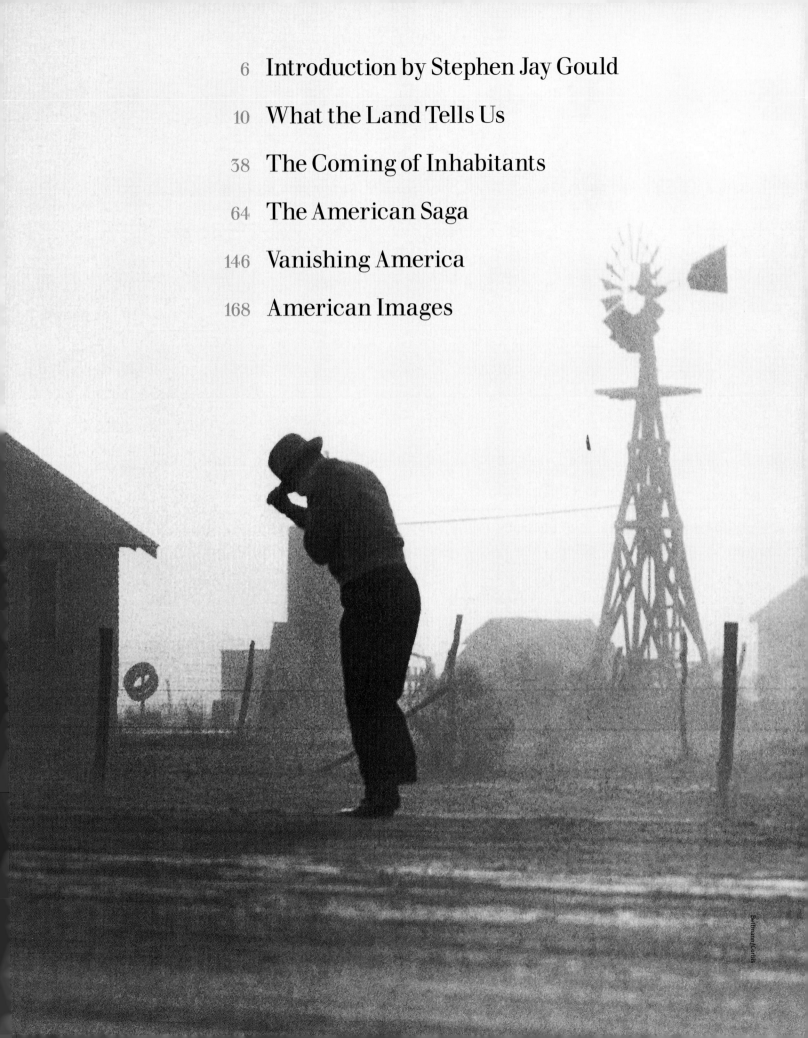

Revealing America

Introduction by Stephen Jay Gould

The traditional history of our schooldays portrayed the fates and times of nations almost entirely in words and pictures about the most visible events and privileged people—tales of rulers and battles, in short. But armies do move on their stomachs, and the changing lives of millions of ordinary people build a more comprehensive and informative history proceeding, often invisibly, beneath the facade of our traditional subjects. We memorized the order of Presidents (as our more unfortunate English colleagues learned the far longer list of kings, and as pupils in Catholic schools struggled with an even lengthier parade of popes). But who knows the inventors of the technologies that altered our societies (and our Earth) far more profoundly than Millard Fillmore or Benjamin Harrison ever impacted our nation? How did agriculture arise? Who made the zipper or the elevator (for we would have no tall buildings, and no cities as we know them, without a mode of rising beyond shank's mare)? And what about the invisible ocean of first drafts and failures beneath the surface of triumphant completion that passes as the pictures of conventional history?

I treasure this book because its pictures present this generally invisible history of common folks, and of hidden aspects behind conventionally great events—an ordinary Indian family rather than Sitting Bull placed alongside a snapshot of Custer, or performing at Buffalo Bill's wild west show; the first try, with interlineations and scratchings out, of a Declaration of Independence, rather than the final document under glass; the chaplain's clock on the *Arizona,* stopped forever by the bombs and fires at Pearl Harbor, rather than ships sinking, men dead, or FDR grimly declaring war. (And to epitomize and symbolize the hope behind every tragedy, that clock, as the old cliché proclaims, is still precisely right twice a day, whereas most clocks never tell the absolutely exact time.)

This book treats change at all scales, from geological millions to human decades, focusing on the vast bulk of things that pass beneath our notice, or that we can't help seeing, but fail to credit or understand. The concept (and actuality) of change fills us with ambivalent feelings, as we love variety, appreciate the necessity of alteration as the way of the world, and even tend (or at least hope) to maintain our traditional equation of change with progress, despite all 20th century horrors from World War I to the Holocaust. And yet, at the same time, we long for stability in our lives, for the stickball courts (the neighbor's wall, and sometimes his broken window) and swimming holes of our youth, while we cannot escape the allure of mythologies about past Golden Ages that never really existed outside our hopes and imaginations. (I, at least, and despite popular nostalgia, largely among folks who had not yet been born at the time, do not remember the 1950's as particularly innocent or idyllic, but rather as a chauvinistic time of cold wars, bomb shelters and racism.)

This book excels in probing these contradictions—in showing us, for example, the icons and artifacts of grandeur for all time-frames and materials—from geological billions in the Grand Canyon; to the sweep of life's history (as symbolized by the touching photo of a fossil dinosaur embryo, obviously dead within its egg more than 65 million years ago); to the broad scale of human history (the remains of the great Anasazi culture, just on the verge of technological greatness, and then gone in a relative moment so many centuries ago); to the finer scale of earlier, and apparently sweeter, versions of the culture we recognize as basically our own (the ghost town of Bodie, California, for example).

Citing more specific examples from the photos in this book, and spanning the full range from triumph to tragedy, consider just a few categories emerging from my own reactions: 1. The profound and the beautiful (again at all scales), from glaciers in steady state, spalling off icebergs as new fields form in valley heads above; to the temperate (not tropical) rainforests of the Pacific Northwest; to Yellowstone and

Throughout the Southwest there are ruins of thousand-year-old civilizations—buildings as high as four stories, ancient pathways. The Anasazi and other cliff-dwelling American Indians thrived, then vanished. Around 1300 this commune in Arizona's Canyon de Chelly, along with others like it, was abandoned. Why? Who were the Anasazi? What tales are in the sandstone?

Monument Valley, slowly eroding the old and revealing the new; to the sweep and beauty of superseded artifacts and practices, from the forest of masts of tall ships in a harbor, to cattle on a drive stretching nearly to the vanishing point of perspective.

2. The grand and the passionate, from the human scale of John Brown on the gallows; to the rude bridge that arched the flood (and marked the first military success of our revolution) at Concord (a reconstruction, of course, as wood rots and nature spoils human hopes for permanency); to the awe of natural forces in Meteor Crater (actually just a tiny stone from the sky, fallen on a geological yesterday, or the resulting landform would have eroded away long ago); or in the recent eruption of Mount St. Helens. (I will never forget my first flight over the site, wondering about hype as we approached from the unaffected side and I saw a perfectly symmetrical "standard" crater, but then awestruck as we flew around and I realized that the back half of the moun-

tain had literally been blown away.)

3. The sweet, smaller and touching that can no longer be—from the two street urchins playing sandlot ball (and obviously using a piece of slate for home plate), to Mark Twain lying in bed and smoking a cigar while reading (an obvious no-no today as both a fire and health hazard, but do we not long for the false comforts of their safety and pleasure?). 4. The enormous swing category of ambiguous images that evoke both visceral warmth and cerebral knowledge of a dark side, either inherent or consequential—a corps of loggers sitting on the trunks of giant felled trees; a speakeasy in times of Prohibition; a family snugly situated in a 1950s bomb shelter; Elvis in a quartet of white boys, who could succeed so smashingly in racist America because they performed in the styles of black musicians who could not gain access to such audiences; the inventive and industrial geniuses Ford and Edison, warm friends and fellow anti-Semites of more than merely passive belief.

The nation is ever changing. Today, the front porch might not be option A for such as the Haven family of Beverly Farms, Massachusetts (seen here circa 1868 with an esteemed guest, Supreme Court Chief Justice Salmon P. Chase, right). TV might lure some inside. For others: new CDs to hear, DVDs to see, 'net games to play.

5. The merely silly or fraudulent in Barnum's country of suckers born each minute, as in the hoaxes of "druidic" monuments spread throughout the American Northeast, and visited (at substantial admission prices) by hordes of the credulous. 6. The ugly side that must be—for example, on Gallows Hill of Salem, where proto-Americans actually hanged women and men accused of witchcraft, until the accusations became too numerous and reached too close to the hearts of too many families of status.

7. The destructive, whether wrought by non-moral nature in her ordinary ways (the Johnstown Flood), or by the fortunate rarity, but ubiquity nonetheless (given the sheer quantity of human beings), of sociopathy (the grassy knoll in Dallas on the day of JFK's assassination). For me, one photo in this category brought all these themes together—scales of destruction, nature vs. culture, the ambivalence of human reaction—as a group of well-dressed women stand on a hilltop and pose themselves for

a photographer, as San Francisco burns in the background during the earthquake of 1906.

And yet (and in conclusion), so much remains—and so much of value—within this swirl. At all scales, as Ecclesiastes tells us, one generation passeth away, but another generation cometh. And so (at human scale), another photo of modern San Francisco shows us a row of Victorian residences that survived in the foreground, with the tall buildings of this most modern and vibrant city in the background. And, as stated before and at geological scale, the natural sculptures of Monument Valley erode and fall away by the same process that forms new pillars of brilliant red sandstone.

I am not a patriot in any conventional sense of flag waving, but I do consider myself an unabashed patriot (and I do mean specifically as a citizen of the United States of America, not only of the world) in my awe and respect for the grandest aspect of our unique nation—so well shown both in the actual photos of this book, and in the guiding theme of ordinary and unnoticed change. We live in the greatest (and even largely successful) experiment in democracy ever attempted on this planet. No other nation has ever, for so long and under democratic premises (however deeply flawed and sometimes even cynically flouted in application), held together in unity across such a blend of climates, economies, ethnicities, traditions, languages and beliefs. And I think that we held through Gettysburg and all other attempts to begin our formal division, because, piece by ordinary piece—symbolized best in this book by two contrasting photos, of the Indian family in traditional garb and the scrubbed Caucasian family outside its new home in the literal Levittown—we have soldered together the most diverse set of peoples and customs into a vibrant amalgam that grants deep truth to a genre usually characterized by false and boastful claims—national mottoes. Ours, however, rings true within all its flaws (like the crack in the Liberty Bell): *E pluribus unum*—One from many.

What
The Land
tells us

What **The Land** tells us

If you trace the Appalachian Mountains, from Canada's Gaspé Peninsula along the Whites and Greens of New England through the Smokies of Tennessee and then to their expiration in Alabama, you will follow a tide of rolling summits and verdant valleys. The Rockies, extending more than 3,000 miles from Alaska to New Mexico, have astonishingly sharp and rugged peaks—whitecaps to the Appalachians' swells. Why are these mountain ranges so different? Other mysteries: Why is there salt on the floor of the desert? Why do parts of the Pacific Northwest resemble the Amazonian rainforest? Why is the water of the big basin in Yellowstone such an unnatural shade of blue? The answers to these questions tell us much about the natural history of our country, how it came to be and where it might be heading. Like the rings of a tree, the shape and size of a mountain betray its age and its experience. The old, worn hills of the northeastern United States suffered a much rougher go with the last ice age than did the upstart Rockies of the West. That salt? Remnant of a once-vast inland sea.

Man has been looking at terrain and trying to decipher its messages for millennia. In the 500s B.C., Greek philosophers posited that moving water helped shape the land and that fossil fish were evidence not only of former life but of bygone oceans. Before he died by probing too near the volcano Vesuvius in A.D. 79, Pliny the Elder assembled all that Rome knew about rocks, minerals and fossils in his 37-volume *Historia Naturalis.* The inquisitiveness of the ancients has been handed down, and the wealth of knowledge has grown higher than Everest. Today's geologist is trained to hear secrets from the subtlest variation in size, color, shape or striation.

But you don't have to be a rock scientist to read the essential natural history of our continent in the world around us. Every landmass and every body of water has a personal history—a tale to tell—and this information is quite often written on its face. When you're through gasping in awe at the Grand Canyon, puzzle it out: What does that river way down there have to do with the stunning cliffs looming above it? Everything, as it happens.

The texture of North America informs who we are. Animals adapted, or didn't, to the land, and man's interaction with varied topographies, climates and beasts affected the success or failure of his settlements. Aspects of the American character evolved in reaction to the ruggedness of terrain. Today, still, the experience in the East differs from the West; Vermonters are different from Californians, owing in part to their unlike environments.

To know ourselves we should know, first, the land.

Most mountain systems have their genesis in the movements of subsurface tectonic plates: At the point of collision, one plate moves down, the other slides over. Folds and faults develop, accompanied by violent volcanism. When things cool off, the mountains, impacted by gravity and erosion, come back to earth. That endgame process started for the Great Smoky Mountains (previous pages) some 300 million years ago. By contrast, the Tetons (opposite), among the youngest of the Rockies, only began to form sometime between four and 13 million years ago and are still rising today.

Many elements shape land. Few do so as vividly as a glacier.

They are still among us, still at work, in the great sheets of Greenland and Antarctica and in pockets of perennial ice from New Zealand to the Himalayas to, at left, mountains south of Juno, Alaska. Mysteries remain concerning the nature of glaciers, but some things are known: They are active, flowing bodies of ice. They destroy and construct, abrading bedrock, depositing debris, leaving a legacy of ponds and lakes, canyons and valleys. Much of the topography we see in the upper half of North America was formed, in some part, by Pleistocene-epoch glaciers, which retreated about 12,000 years ago. Even parts of the country never covered by ice were affected, as the melt flooded what is now Florida.

Of course I had not been at the crater one day before I *knew* [it] was an impact crater."

That was the report of Daniel Moreau Barringer, a Philadelphia mining engineer, who first visited the mammoth hole in northern Arizona in 1902 and quickly surmised that it hadn't been caused by a volcano but by some extraterrestrial element. Turns out he was right, and in 1920 this was the first crater on Earth to be recognized as having been caused by impact.

How it happened: Nearly 50,000 years ago a massive meteorite as much as 150 feet across smashed into the planet at approximately 40,000 miles per hour. The sphere exploded with a force greater than 20 million tons of TNT, creating a crater 700 feet deep and 4,000 feet across. Barringer's Standard Iron Company spent more than two decades searching in vain for the giant iron ball that he figured was buried beneath the floor of the crater. We now know that the meteorite was obliterated.

Jim Wark/Peter Arnold

Daniel J. Cox/Natural Exposures

Jim Corwin/Stock Solution

Here is neither Africa nor South America. These rainforests inhabit Alaska and Washington.

A rainforest is defined as having an annual rainfall of at least 100 inches; in Washington's Hoh (right) and Alaska's Tongass (above), there can be twice that. These forests, rare in temperate zones, were created by prevailing warm winds from the Pacific, which, forced upward by coast-hugging mountains, cooled rapidly and turned to moisture. The hushed lushness of the rainforest is multi-layered. The top is marked by the giant Sitka spruce and western hemlock. Hoh, unlike Tongass, has a middle tier of deciduous trees. The floor of both is a profusion of shrubs, ferns and mosses. Fauna thrive at every level.

Nothing is so emblematic of the American West as Monument Valley.

The Southwest is dominated by the Colorado Plateau, which is actually not a plateau but a 130,000-square-mile assemblage of plateaus, mountains and canyons ranging in elevation from 2,000 feet to more than 12,700 feet. Breathtaking vistas are everywhere, in the Red Rock country near the Grand Canyon (right) and in Monument Valley (above), which is actually not a valley but a somewhat desolate 2,000-square-mile flat landscape in Arizona and Utah, interrupted by buttes, spires and arches that can reach a thousand feet into the air. Made of ancient deposits of sandstone, rock and shale, these monoliths were slowly pushed up from the earth and then endured the withering effects of erosion to become magnificent, richly hued formations. Perhaps the most evocative images of Monument Valley are to be found in the movies of John Ford, who set many of his classic westerns there.

George Steinmetz (2)

Man is seldom willing to coexist with a natural landscape, particularly if he has the power to modify it," states an article on the Everglades in *The Encyclopedia Americana*.

There is only one Everglades: a 4,000-square-mile basin that was once at the bottom of the sea. Continuously flooded and drained during the most recent ice age, the region, which covers much of southern Florida, is today home to the "River of Grass," mangrove swamps, saltwater marshes, "tree islands" of willow and (above) bald cypress. It is an ecosystem in which everything is connected and the flow of water is everything. Throughout the 20th century that flow was repeatedly diverted for agricultural and other interests. The effects were devastating. Whether this vast but vulnerable wilderness can survive the needs of an expanding human population remains to be seen.

Mount St. Helens used to be known as the Fuji of America because of its dazzling symmetrical beauty.

That all changed on May 18, 1980, with one of the greatest eruptions ever in North America. For two months, scientists had monitored activity in the Washington volcano, dormant since 1857. Rising magma was causing its north flank to swell a shocking five feet a day. The bulge was more than 450 feet on May 18 when a magnitude-5.1 earthquake launched the biggest recorded landslide in the history of the world, followed by a lateral blast of superheated stone, ash and poisonous gas that extended nearly 20 miles. At the same time, a vertical eruption 15 miles high blew volcanic ash eastward around the globe.

The world around Mount St. Helens was forever altered. The volcanic cone was blown away, leaving a horseshoe-shaped crater and a peak one seventh shorter at 8,363 feet. About one cubic mile of Mount St. Helens was hurled into the air. Fifty-seven people and thousands of animals were killed. Ten million trees were felled. Avalanche debris, mudslides and ash wreaked havoc on houses, roads and railways.

And then, rebirth.

The pre-eruption landscape of Mount St. Helens had been one of dense coniferous forests and clear streams and lakes. The photo at near right was taken four years after the explosion; at far right, 20 years after. Both speak to nature's unquenchable need to reinvent itself. Indeed, the area affords a perfect opportunity to study ecological succession and the manner in which habitat may be revitalized. For the record: Mount St. Helens remains a potentially active and dangerous volcano.

Gary Braasch (2)

Chuck Place

A few thousand years ago, in a far wetter climate, Death Valley was filled with water 30 feet deep.

But the climate warmed and the rainfall dwindled, till finally the waters there evaporated into a briny soup. The salts—which are 95 percent table salt— crystallized, coating the muddy lakebed to a depth of five feet. At Devil's Golf Course in Death Valley (right), the salt formed rugged crusts. By contrast, Utah's Bonneville Salt Flats (above), a remnant of a huge 30,000-year-old lake, has a very smooth surface, formed by regular evaporation and flooding. By summer's end the 100-square-mile flats have been baked to a concrete-like hardness and thus, since 1935, have been the setting for numerous land-speed records. Just to the northeast, the Great Salt Lake is another organic remnant of this ancient inland sea.

Fred Hirschmann

Yellowstone is an otherworldly land of geysers and hot springs that hide a secret.

What you see tells a tale of what's beneath. Volcanic action heats rock just a few hundred feet below the surface, and this in turn creates all manner of thermal spectacle in thousands of steaming hot springs and hundreds of geysers, plus bubbling mudpots and fumaroles. Old Faithful erupts every 88 minutes, and the warm water of the basins, including Grand Prismatic Spring (right), allows vivid blue, yellow and green algae to grow year-round.

Here's the disquieting secret. Yellowstone sits upon a 2,000° lake of molten rock, an underground pressure cooker 50 miles long and 30 wide. For at least a few million years, since magma burned a hole under ancient Wyoming's bedrock, Yellowstone had periodically disgorged a small ocean of basalt lava in eruptions hundreds of times worse than any recent volcanic explosion. Subterranean Yellowstone amounts to a volcano the size of Rhode Island that, if it were to erupt in our modern age, would rain ash on Ashland, Kansas. In the 20th century, there was a three-foot swelling of the ground's surface. Magma stirring. Yellowstone last blew more than 600,000 years ago. Is it due?

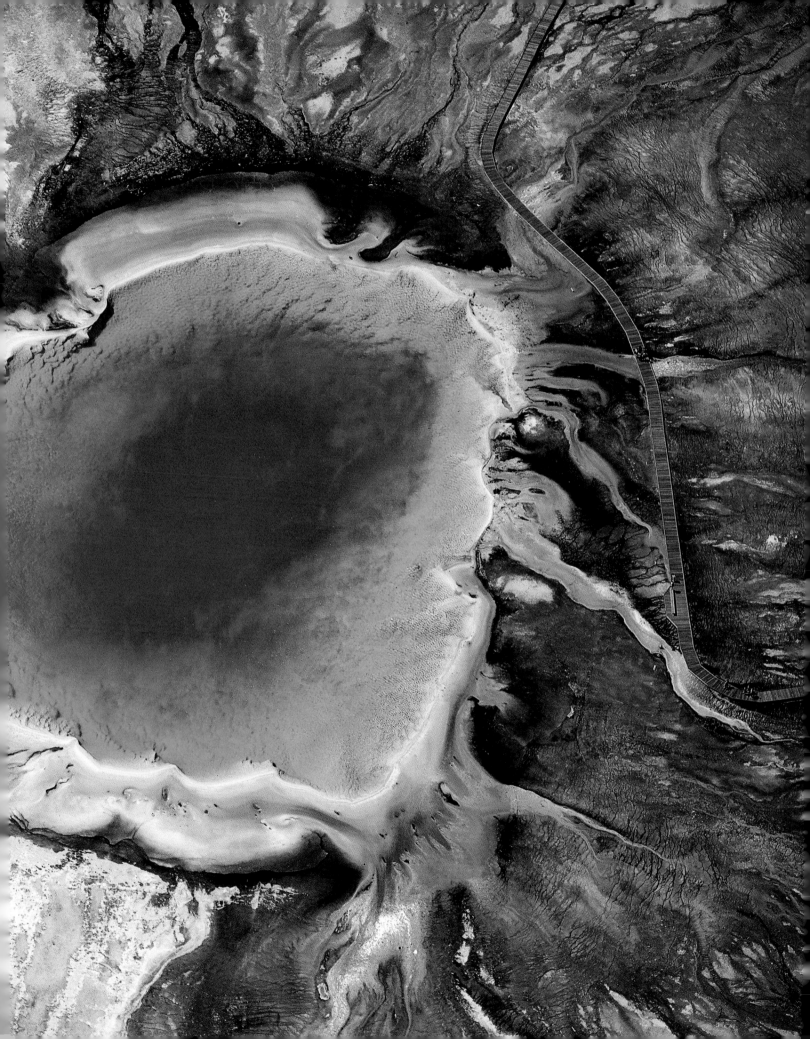

The Grand Canyon is carved deep by the master hand ...

it is all time inscribing the naked rock; it is the book of earth."

Two billion years ago, events conspired to create the incomparable Grand Canyon. Tectonic mayhem, water, erosion and "deposition," the formation of rock from sundry materials, began to converge in a mysterious, endless arabesque. Then 60 million years ago, two geological plates collided. A huge plateau was upthrust, and the Colorado River—the tool in Donald Culross Peattie's "master hand"—began its exquisite sculpture. The result, after six million years, is 277 miles long and a mile deep. Nowhere else exists such a profound record of time's passage, indelibly etched in the exposed rock of canyon walls.

The word "awesome" might well be reserved
for the Grand Canyon. When first confronting it,
people typically dissolve into a preverbal state.
There are so many stupendous elements—
constantly in flux owing to the shifting sun—
that the mind struggles to process them.

NASA

Beringia: It wasn't just a bridge but a vast plain of tundra 1,000 miles wide, linking there to here.

During the last ice age, oceans receded when glaciers stole their water. Slowly, Asia, which was already populated by man, and North America—which was not—became a single landmass as terra firma emerged in the northern seas. The "bridge" reached from what is now Barrow, Alaska, down to the Aleutian Islands—580,000 square miles in all, twice the size of Texas (all the water in the photo above, plus much more, was land). New evidence shows that melting ice and rising seas didn't sink the bridge until as recently as 11,000 years ago. Today, the shortest open-water expanse between Alaska and Siberia is the Bering Strait, 55 miles across. Midway lie two land-bridge remnants, the Diomede Islands. At right is Big Diomede, as seen from the U.S., with Siberia distant; the international date line splits the islands. In a bygone era, traffic was constant at this passage.

Fred Bruemmer/Peter Arnold

The coming of
Inhabitants

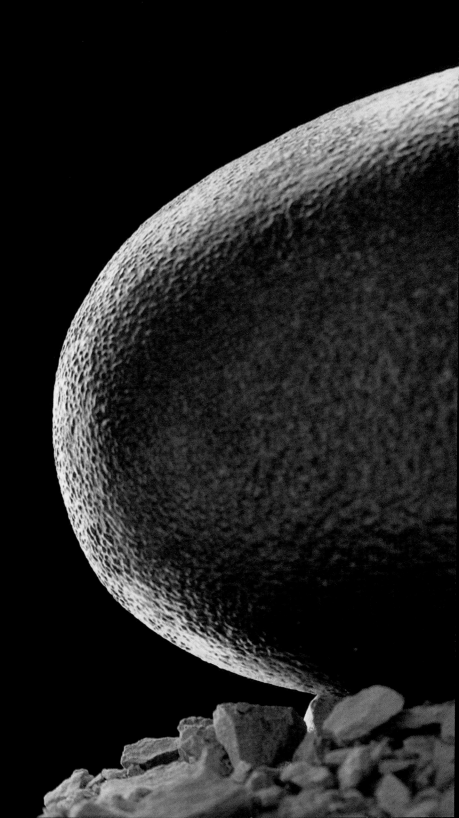

The coming of **Inhabitants**

Two hundred million years ago, according to a theory fathered by German meteorologist Alfred Wegener in 1912, there was Pangaea, the supercontinent. Jurassic beasts roamed its hills and plains, and then, slowly, the gigantic landmass began to tear itself apart.

After more than 60 million years of continental drift, Laurasia, heading north, separated itself from Gondwanaland. India and another huge island that included both Antarctica and Australia were floating free. These new continents were still on the move, as tectonic plates supporting them continued to shift, move apart, sometimes crash together—for example, when the isle of India rejoined the mainland. Laurasia finally split, with Eurasia spiraling away to the northeast and North America going west. Each boat floated its own animals. They were earthen arks bearing dinosaurs.

Sixty-five million years ago, something happened. Perhaps an immense asteroid—or a fierce asteroid shower—kicked up so much debris that the planet was plunged into darkness, a yearlong winter. Perhaps violent volcanism was the cause. The debate rages today, with one certainty: Something killed the dinosaurs in what amounted to a heartbeat.

Species that had been hanging in the shadow of the dinosaurs could now emerge and evolve. Rodents came down from the trees, reptiles came out of the swamps. The earliest large mammals made their presence known. Perhaps 20 million years ago the first hominoids developed, and more than three million years ago humans were born in Africa.

North and South America were largely immune to development on the other continents; each was an island to the other. And so, in the past 300,000 years, while Swanscombe Man and Steinheim Man and Solo Man and Rhodesian Man and Neanderthal Man and Cro-Magnon Man were having massive impacts elsewhere, the wildlife of the Americas evolved according to its own rules. As recently as 15,000 years ago, the animal population of North America resembled that of East Africa, with lions, cheetahs, saber-toothed cats, mammoths and descendants of camels doing fine.

The Pleistocene ice age had a dual impact. As Arctic conditions crept south, the new climate proved unsuitable for some species, but of much greater long-term consequence: The land bridge formed between Siberia and Alaska. Across it walked bighorn sheep, musk ox, wolverines, bison, beavers, grizzly bears, assorted other species—and humans. These first Americans very quickly worked their way south and east, and by the time the land bridge closed, they were sufficient in number to survive, settle, hunt, prosper, colonize, thrive. To dominate.

Eye-opening discoveries: In the late 1970s dino hunter Jack Horner found evidence of a new genus of duckbill in Montana. His yield included rare bones of several babies (previous pages—a reconstruction of a hatchling). If Horner is correct that the nesting area proves dinosaurs nurtured their young, then this would imply behavior more closely related to warm-blooded animals than cold-blooded reptiles. Also in the 1970s, in Colorado, Jim Jensen found pieces of a giant he called *Ultrasaurus* (opposite). This vegetarian, believed to be 100 feet long, established that American dinos were as big as anyone's.

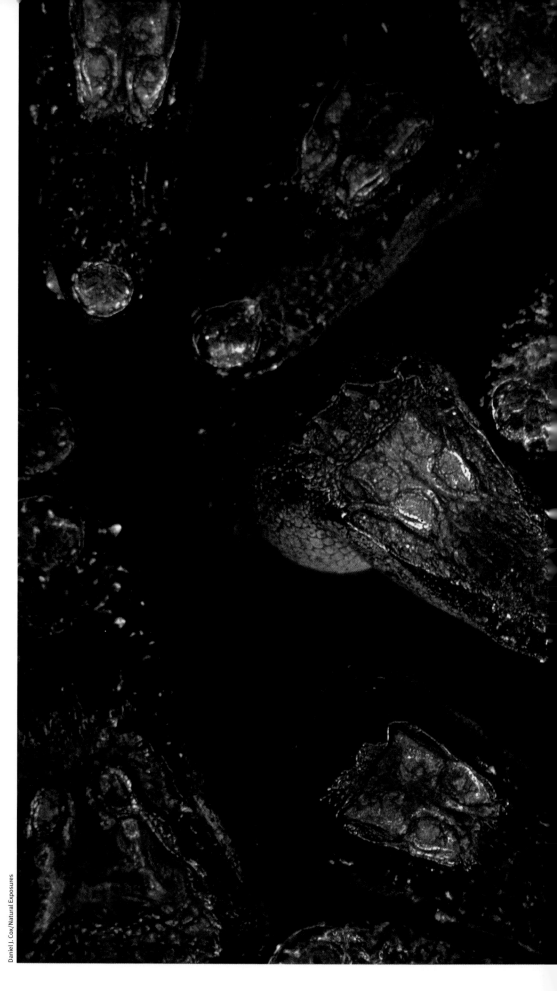

The American alligator has been here for 20 million years.

But it is not a relic of the dinosaurs, a "living fossil." A member of the crocodilian family, this reptile may be linked to creatures from 50 million years ago, and resembles animals that lived as long as 100 million years ago, during the late Cretaceous period—a very different world from today, yet with certain natural parallels.

Alligator populations suffered a serious blow in the last century when hide-hunters killed countless of them for human accessories like handbags and belts. The Endangered Species Act of 1973 curtailed most of the poaching, and the great beasts have made a decent comeback.

Art Wolfe/Image Bank

When thou seest an eagle, thou seest a portion of genius; lift up thy head."

Chosen for its longevity, strength and majesty, the splendid creature referred to by William Blake has been the national symbol since the Great Seal of the United States was adopted in 1782. Once severely endangered, the bald eagle has been a model of ecological recovery. These birds mate for life, and the couple will often continue to live in the same nest, which can become enormous. One in Ohio was 9½ feet wide and 20 feet deep. Another weighed two tons. The marvel of the creature seen above, the musk ox, may be that we coexist with it at all. Like the alligator on the preceding pages, the musk ox is a representative of another, earlier time. Now resident in Alaska, the musk ox was a Pleistocene-era Siberian émigré—easy to believe when considering its hair, which may be the longest of any wild animal.

Jack A. Barrie/Bruce Coleman

Bighorn sheep are "the bravest of all the Sierra mountaineers."

John Muir's remark would surely ring true to anyone familiar with the bighorn. It is another species that arrived long ago from Asia. Once here, an interesting change happened: The beefy Rocky Mountain variety (above) can weigh 300 pounds, but a different subspecies, the desert bighorn (left), tops off at 200 pounds. In a hot, dry climate, it has grown smaller, and carries a lighter coat and longer legs. The coyote (right), a North American native that is sort of a cross between a wolf and a fox, has long been linked with the West, but in the 20th century it began spreading eastward and now thrives in every state but Hawaii. The coyote, too, has been altered in its migration. Western ones seldom exceed 35 pounds, but the eastern version may weigh twice that much. How did this happen so quickly? The prevalent opinion holds that coyotes mated with wolves along the way.

Bats and flying squirrels are common mammals but rarely seen because they inhabit a nocturnal world.

Bats, like the spear-nosed ones above, are the only mammals possessed of true flight. They are often misunderstood, owing to horror stories and concerns about rabies. Actually, bats rarely transmit the disease. They are, in fact, quite beneficial because of the hordes of mosquitoes and other insects they consume. Flying squirrels (opposite) are found over much of the country. Of course, these docile, silky-haired rodents don't really fly. Rather, they spread the furry membrane between their legs and glide, even as far as 160 feet.

Kennewick Man's skeleton ignites different kinds of controversy.

In 1996 a skull was found near the Columbia River outside Kennewick, Washington. Subsequent investigation turned up a nearly complete human skeleton. Aspects of the bones were said by some scientists to be more Caucasoid than Native American, and when first-round radiocarbon dating established an age of 9,500 years, theories of migration patterns were challenged. Could Europeans have been here as early as Asians? All questions were put on hold when local tribes petitioned to rebury the bones. Kennewick Man's skeleton was seized by authorities, and his fate will be determined in court.

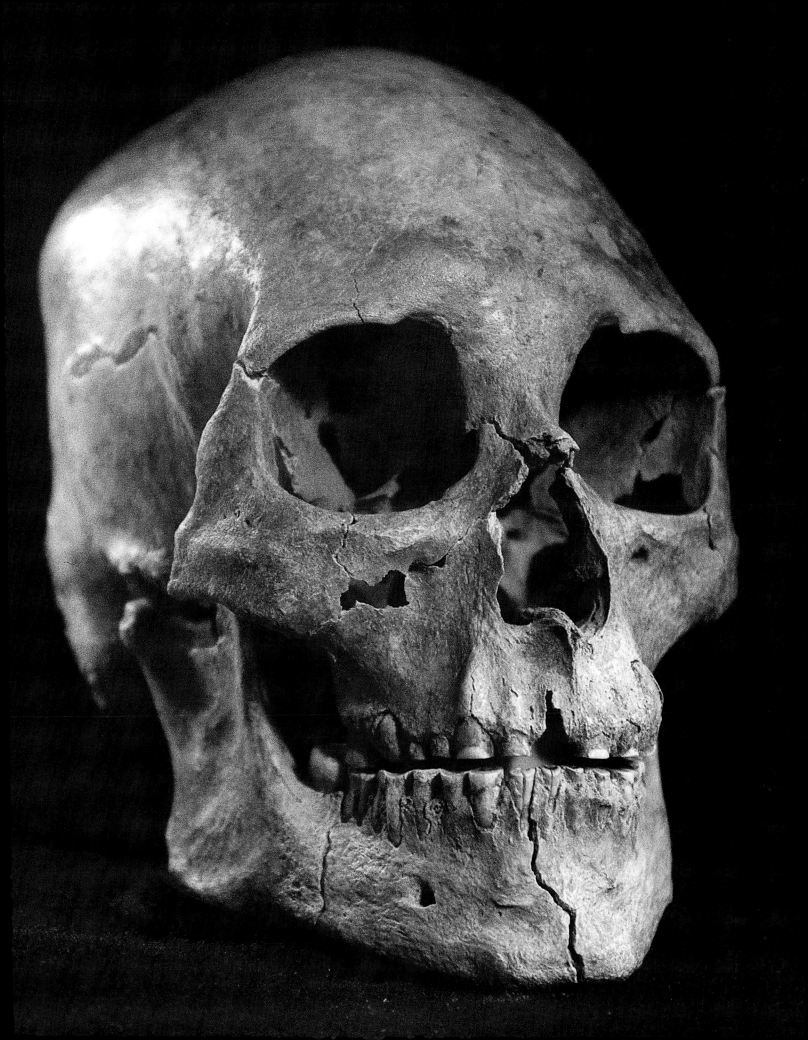

The mounds, which are found coast-to-coast, sometimes contain bones. They always contain mysteries.

While American history is well documented, America's prehistory is often ignored. Whatever the implications of Kennewick Man, humans were firmly established in the New World thousands of years before the white man's arrival. They built civilizations from Alaska to Georgia. Eventually, the early Indians' hunter-gatherer lifestyle grew in sophistication, as evidenced by found tools, artifacts and earthworks. Most spectacular among the legacies are thousands of mounds throughout the U.S. Some were burial places (above, in Mississippi), some marked sacred sites. The Great Serpent Mound near Hillsboro, Ohio (right), is the largest effigy mound in the world, averaging 20 feet wide by five high and running a quarter mile tip-to-tail. The Adena culture that constructed it began building mounds about 700 B.C.

The Anasazi were the Athenians of the Southwest.

They had planned communities and roadways, crafted pottery and jewelry, irrigated fields. Their ancestors 6,000 years earlier were migratory hunters who began to master techniques for grinding seeds and, slowly, evolved into agrarians. By the end of the first millennium the Anasazi were farming in valleys and on mesas, and dwelling in cliffs. Not long thereafter the culture's gleaming Pueblo Bonito rose from the desert floor (right). The three-acre, multi-story edifice in the shadow of New Mexico's Chaco Canyon had 660 rooms and 32 large "kivas" for communal gatherings. A thousand Anasazi lived in Pueblo Bonito until the mid-13th century, then they were gone. Were the Anasazi wiped out by an invading tribe? Did they succumb to drought, famine, the stresses of overpopulation? We will probably never know.

They left behind no written record, only small clues.

Petroglyphs (like these on Newspaper Rock in Arizona's Petrified Forest National Park) depict daily life. Clearly, animals were important to these people as symbols as well as sources of food. But beyond tantalizing hints in the cryptic cryptograms, there is little. We can't even know what these early Indians were really called. The term *Anasazi* means "Enemy Ancestors" in the Navajo language; much of the scant Anasazi record comes from that tribe and other invaders (some of whom wrote on Newspaper Rock as well). The Anasazi, for their part, left or were driven from their settlements, and by 1300 had all but disappeared. Ethnographers and anthropologists have determined that the remnants of this once great nation became the Pueblo Indians, who still inhabit the Southwest.

Gary Braasch

So who really *was* the first from the Old World to reach the New?

The strongest claim as we sail into the third millennium belongs to the Vikings, who unquestionably reached Newfoundland and established "Vinland" at the turn of the first millennium. (In a page from *Eric's Saga,* above, North Americans are described as "small and evil-looking" with "large eyes and broad cheekbones.") But then there's the case of St. Brendan. In 1976, Tim Severin sailed from Ireland to Canada in a replica of an ancient skin-covered boat (right) to prove that the storied 6th-century Irish monk could have made the voyage.

Do the chambers hold ancient secrets or evidence of recent tomfoolery?

Scattered through the Northeast are scores of "mystery caves" and "sacramental sites." They indicate either that other Europeans did indeed precede the Vikings to North America, or that someone's got a bill of goods to sell. In the Massachusetts towns of Danvers, Upton and Hopkinton, Celtic-type rock huts called beehives have been discovered. Up the road in Salem, New Hampshire, the Mystery Hill Caves are a series of "beehives" that certainly do resemble those of the Fir-Bolgs and the Tuatha De Danaan Celts, who thrived hundreds of years before the coming of Christ. In North Salem, New York, the argument is made that the giant boulder seen above simply could not have been placed so carefully upon its standing stones by glacial action. It *must* have Celtic significance. And a well-known set of chambers a bit farther north, in Putnam County (right), is said by some to be traceable to ancient Europe. Others say they're traceable to the Revolutionary War, when they were used as storage depots. No matter how strong the evidence presented, people will believe what they choose.

Granger Collection

Sailing an ocean blue, an Italian working for Spain arrived in 1492.

Christopher Columbus (above) did not, of course, discover America; he never even stepped upon the North American mainland. Having set out for Japan and India, he delivered Cuba and Hispaniola—or, in the words of historian Daniel J. Boorstin, Columbus "promised a gold mine, and only found a wilderness." A successor, Juan Ponce de León, pushed farther into that wilderness, landing in Florida in 1513. That same year, Vasco Núñez de Balboa reached the Pacific, and not long after, Hernando Cortés arrived in Mexico. What is now the United States was about to be invaded on all sides.

In 1565 yet another Spanish explorer, Pedro Menéndez de Avilés, founded a settlement in northeastern Florida on the Atlantic and called it St. Augustine. That town stands today as the oldest permanent white settlement in the country.

Nathan Farb

The **American** saga

The **American** saga

Even in the prelude to nationhood, America was a melting pot, as the Spanish were followed in their efforts at colonization by British, French, German, Dutch, Irish, Finnish and Swedish immigrants. Many came in search of wealth, others for individual or religious freedom. Their aspirations informed what became known as "the American character."

Danger and the prospect of premature death were constant for the earliest settlers from Europe. Sir Walter Raleigh's 1585 attempt to establish a British settlement on Roanoke Island, off what is now North Carolina, failed, with the colonists returning to England the next year. Raleigh tried again in 1587, sending 91 men, 17 women and nine children. Their fate remains one of America's eeriest mysteries. When an English ship next visited Roanoke in August 1590, the sailors found no traces of the colony, only the letters CRO carved into one tree, the word CROATOAN into another. The colonists' intentions had been to travel north to Chesapeake Bay and establish a community. Perhaps they did so, and ran afoul of Indians. Or perhaps they were taken in by the friendly Croatoan Indians to the south (even today, the Lumbee Indians of southeastern North Carolina maintain that they have Lost Colonists in their family tree). The truth remains unknown, and probably ever will.

A group of more than 100 Englishmen did finally settle near Chesapeake Bay in 1607, naming their community after the reigning British king, James I. Not long after, in 1620, the ship *Mayflower* transported religious refugees to what would become Plymouth Colony in Massachusetts. The colonial period of American history, which would extend more than a century and a half, saw Dutch and Swedish colonies established in what are now the states of New York, New Jersey and Delaware, though these communities were subsequently brought under British control. Things that today seem quintessentially American were contributed by various European cultures and ethnicities. The Finns and Swedes built the country's first log cabins near the mouth of the Delaware River before 1640.

This mixed group of rugged, intrepid colonists, which eventually stretched from Maine (then part of Massachusetts) to Georgia, held some values in common. Among these were a reverence for the work ethic and notions of libertarianism. William Penn's theology is instructive. His Pennsylvania colony, founded in 1681, wasn't intended as a sanctuary just for Quakers but as a place where people of all faiths could enjoy religious liberty.

In other words, America wasn't like Europe generally or England specifically. And when England decided to make its colonies get back into line, something was bound to happen.

Something did.

This is what it might have looked like in May 1607 to 105 adventurous men who would make land here and create Jamestown, the first permanent English settlement in America. They had seen "faire meddowes and goodly tall trees" along the Virginia coast; would that they had stopped at one of those sites. "James Towne" was swampy and its drinking water impure. For years the colonists endured dysentery, hunger, fires and hostile Indians. Previous pages: Shortly after midnight on April 19, 1775, a silversmith named Paul Revere hastened along the green of Lexington, Massachusetts. Later that morning a shot would ring out, a minuteman fall dead, and nothing would ever again be the same.

Men feared witches and burned women."

Louis Brandeis wrote those words in 1927, adding, "It is the function of speech to free men from the bondage of irrational fears." It was a century and a half after the principle of free speech in a democracy had begun to set men free; the incident to which he alluded, long a dark mark on the soul of the country, had occurred many years before the founding of the nation. The Puritans came to the Massachusetts Bay Colony as persecuted men and women. In the late 1600s they turned persecutors. Suspicion and unwarranted terror were rife, and civil magistrates reacted irrationally, sending scores of "witches" to prison. Of 200 arrested in 1692 in Salem, 17 died in mean jails like the one at left. On Gallows Hill (opposite), 19 were hanged, then thrown into a burial pit. (While local legend has this as "the hanging tree," it is, in fact, not old enough.) In 1957, in an era when witch-hunts were again a topic of discussion, the Massachusetts legislature posthumously exonerated some of the witches of Salem. As recently as 2001, descendants of five women executed for witchcraft 300 years ago were again before a Massachusetts tribunal, pressuring the lawmakers to proclaim the women's innocence by name. The Salem witchcraft trials will never die.

Nina Leen (2)

Here once the embattled farmers stood, And fired the shot heard round the world."

Emerson composed his *Concord Hymn* for a ceremony commemorating events in his hometown that, a half century earlier, had begun the colonies' march toward nationhood. On April 18, 1775, British redcoats had, under cover of night, come out of Boston seeking rebel arms they knew to be stashed in rural Concord, among other places. In Lexington at dawn on the 19th they met resistance in the form of a ragtag militia of "minutemen" — ready to respond in a minute — who had been

forewarned by Paul Revere and other riders. The disagreement that had led to the standoff in Lexington was, by that point, absolute and immutable. The radicals' gripe was that the colonies were being harshly governed and unfairly taxed by England. The British opinion held that London ruled the world on both sides of the Atlantic, and any gun-bearing rebels were criminals against the crown. These philosophical differences came to a violent point on the Lexington green (opposite) when several colonials were killed and, later that morning, on the North Bridge at Concord (right and above), where the patriots fired their muskets, killing three British soldiers. Soon minutemen from neighboring villages swarmed to Concord. Practicing guerilla warfare, they shot from behind stone walls, hectoring the British retreat. By day's end, there were 273 British casualties. The American Revolution was on.

George Washington's ascent to fame began at age 21.

In October 1753, Washington, a major in the Virginia militia, was sent by the governor with a message to a French outpost near Lake Erie warning against encroachment on land already claimed by Britain. The journey from Williamsburg to Fort Le Boeuf was 360 miles as the crow flies, but twice that on horseback. Some 25 miles along, Washington came to Williams' Landing (left), which at the time had a ferry wharf, and where today old wagon tracks are still visible. He returned in January and wrote a vivid account of his arduous trip and the defiant French reply. The French and Indian War was in the offing, and Washington's tale earned him a name. Elfreth's Alley (opposite) had already existed for half a century when Washington made his trek. The Philadelphia byway, America's oldest residential street, looked much like this when Ben Franklin went a-walkin'.

The principles of Jefferson are the definitions and axioms of free society."

Such was the opinion of Abraham Lincoln. Thomas Jefferson was born on the family farm in central Virginia in 1743 to a world of privilege. But he had a typical country boy's inquisitiveness—in spades. Indeed, here is how James Parton described the adult Jefferson: "A gentleman of thirty-two who could calculate an eclipse, survey an estate, tie an artery, plan an edifice, try a cause, break a horse, dance a minuet and play the violin." The education of such a wonder began early. He was tutored from 1748 to 1752 in the building at left, near Richmond. From age nine he began to receive a solid grounding in the classics. At 16 he entered William and Mary, where he studied with George Wythe (inset), the country's first law professor. Wythe would be a lifelong friend and mentor to Jefferson, and would sign his protégé's Declaration of Independence.

A Declaration by the Representatives of the UNITED STATES OF AMERICA, in General Congress assembled.

When in the course of human events it becomes necessary for one people to dissolve the political bands which have connected them with another, and to ~~assume among the powers of the earth the~~ as-sume among the powers of the earth the separate and equal station to which the laws of nature & of nature's god entitle them, a decent respect to the opinions of mankind requires that they should declare the causes which impel them to the separation.

We hold these truths to be self-evident, ~~sacred & undeniable~~ that all men are created equal ~~& independent~~ that ~~from that equal creation they derive~~ they are endowed by their creator with ~~rights~~ inherent & inalienable rights, that among these are the ~~preservation of~~ life, & liberty, & the pursuit of happiness; that to secure these rights, go-vernments are instituted among men, deriving their just powers from the consent of the governed; that whenever any form of government ~~shall~~ becomes destructive of these ends, it is the right of the people to alter or to abolish it, & to institute new government, laying it's foundation on such principles & organising it's powers in such form, as to them shall seem most likely to effect their safety & happiness. prudence indeed will dictate that governments long established should not be changed for light & transient causes: and accordingly all experience hath shewn that mankind are more disposed to suffer while evils are sufferable, than to right themselves by abolishing the forms to which they are accustomed. but when a long train of abuses & usurpations [begun at a distinguished period, &] pursuing invariably the same object, evinces a design to ~~subject~~ reduce them + under absolute Despotism, it is their right, it is their duty, to throw off such ~~government~~ + & to provide new guards for their future security. such has been the patient sufferance of these colonies; & such is now the necessity which constrains them to expunge their former systems of government. the history of the present King of Great Britain. is a history of unremitting injuries and ~~usurpations,~~ appears no solitary fact to contra-

My mother died about eight o'clock this morning in the 57th year of her age."

So reported Thomas Jefferson in his journal on March 31, 1776. The dispassionate words belie an intense sadness that turned to depression and immobilized him for six weeks. Finally emerging from his mourn, Jefferson threw himself into a period of frenzied and brilliant creativity that resulted in his masterworks, the Virginia constitution and the Declaration of Independence. To be sure, the latter was not the work of one man's mind, great as the mind may have been. Jefferson, part of a five-man committee, sketched the Declaration, then produced a "fair" copy he called the "original Rough draught." This was revised first by John Adams, then Ben Franklin, then by the full committee (their 47 alterations are included on the copy at left). On June 28 the committee presented to the Continental Congress, which four days later voted for independence. The Congress made 39 more revisions, then voted for adopting the document on July 4. A subsequent draft (right) was used by John Dunlap to make the first printed version of the work; copies of the "Dunlap Broadside" were hurried to colonial leaders. George Washington received his in New York City and on July 9 ordered it read to the American army.

The importance of the Lewis and Clark expedition lay on the level of imagination ..."

" ... it was drama, the enactment of a myth that embodied the future," wrote Henry Nash Smith. When Jefferson took office in 1801, he sought to expand the nation. For one thing, he felt that a water passage existed to the Pacific; for another, Jefferson, the imperialist, craved property. Like other Virginia planters, he made his living with tobacco, wheat and slavery, which demanded new land. He tapped Meriwether Lewis (near left) to lead the trek. Lewis signed on his former army officer, the resolute William Clark. The 8,000-mile journey opened the way to the West. Here, the Missouri, Lewis and Clark's highway to the Rockies, winds through Montana.

is black and the iris of a silver white. the under jaw
exceeds the upper; and the mouth opens to
great extent, folding like that of the herring. it
has no teeth. the abdomen is obtuse and
smooth; in this differing from the herring, shad
anchovey &c of the Malacapterygious order
and class Clupea, to which howe-
-ver I think it more nearly allyed
than to any other altho' it has not
theer accute and serrate abdomen
and the under jaw exceed- -ing the
upper. the scales of this little fish
are so small and thin that without
manute inspection you would
suppose they had none. they are
felled with roes of a pure white
colour and have scercely any perceptl
-able alimentary duct. I found them
best when cooked in Indian Stilo, which
is by roasting) a number of them toge=
-ther on a wooden spit without any prea-
-vious prepar- -ation whatever. they are
so fat that they require no aditional
sauce, and I think them superior to any
flesh I ever tasted, even more delicate and
luscious than the white fish of the Lakes
which have heretofore formed my standert
of excellence among the fishes. I have herd
the fresh anchovey much extalled but I hope I shall
be pardoned for beliieving this quit as good. the
bones are so soft and fine that they form no obstruction
in eating this fish.

Jefferson, the man of parts, burned to know the flora and fauna of the unseen West. To that end, he gave the great frontiersman Lewis the wherewithal to record his experience. Lewis spent two solid years with Jefferson as his secretary, and it was from him that he learned how to be a writer. As historian Stephen E. Ambrose says of Lewis's style: "He sharpened his descriptive powers. He learned how to catch a reader up in his own response to events and places ..." Lewis had also been schooled by experts in the fields of navigation, geography and American Indians. Scholars in Philadelphia had taught him the intricacies of classifying plants and animals. It was a thorough preparation for an unprecedented endeavor, and yielded Lewis's immortal journal, excerpted here.

Grouse are about short and eye. Cock Cock which on the and hood Mountains to the Mountain the Columbia the Great falls they go in large or singularly hide hide remarkably close when pursued. Short flights &c.

the feathers about its head pointed and stiff some hairs the base of the beak. feathers fine and stiff about the ears. This is a faint likeness of the of the plains or Heath the first of those fowls we met with was Missouri below in the neighbor= of the Rocky and from which pass between and Rapids gangs Gangues and make

The Large Black & White Pheasant is peculiar to that portion of the Rocky Mountains watered by the Columbia River. at least we did not see them untill we reached the waters of that river, nor since we have left those Mountains. they are about the size of a well grown hen. the contour of the bird is much that of the redish brown Pheasant common to our country. the tail is proportionably as long and is composed of 18 feathers of equal length, of a uniform dark brown tiped with black. the feather of the body are of a dark brown black and white. the black

is that which most predominates, and white feathers

The Oregon Trail was 10 miles wide in some places. In others, a wagon could just squeeze by.

In the early 19th century, fur traders and mountain men were among the brave few (like Lewis and Clark) who blazed a trail to the West. But in the 1840s one of the greatest voluntary migrations in history got under way when midwestern farmers became intrigued by the richness of Oregon's Willamette Valley. After preparing all winter for the 2,000-mile, half-year journey, families usually gathered in small parties at Independence, Missouri, near the great river. Some 300,000 emigrants made the grinding trip, usually in covered wagons pulled by oxen. Women would fill the butter churn and hang it off the back of the wagon; the road would be rough enough to process a bit of butter for supper. Chimney Rock (right) in western Nebraska, visible from 40 miles away, was a key landmark for pioneers. The clan below rested at midday in the foothills of the Rockies.

Abraham Lincoln his hand and pen/He will be good but God knows when."

Lincoln composed that charming couplet as a child. He had, of course, been born in Kentucky, but by the time the boy was seven, his family—saddled with a faulty land title and uncomfortable with that state's slavery—moved to Indiana, near Pigeon Creek, in what is now Spencer County (seen here). It was an unwelcoming place, remote and demanding. In an 1860 autobiography, Lincoln would write: "Abraham, though very young, was large of his age, and had an axe put into his hands at once; and from that till within his twenty-third year, he was almost constantly handling that most useful instrument—less, of course, in plowing and harvesting seasons." The fence above represents the sort of endeavor that lent the Rail Splitter his sobriquet.

By the 1830s, Lincoln had relocated to Illinois, where he developed an interest in politics. While a member of the state legislature, he was urged to study law by John T. Stuart, a Springfield attorney. Lincoln sometimes walked the 20 miles from his home in New Salem to Stuart's office to borrow law books. In 1836, Lincoln received his law license and moved to Springfield as the junior partner in the law firm Stuart and Lincoln. Because the Springfield courts were inactive for most of the year, he traveled the 8,700-square-mile circuit, often on horseback, following a judge from county to county. Lincoln practiced law in the Decatur courthouse seen above and opposite. His skills as a lawyer made him known throughout Illinois. Lincoln was able to present a graspable case to an unschooled jury or to argue a complex issue with a savvy judge. And the man's integrity was never in dispute. This photo of Honest Abe was taken in Chicago in 1857.

Yours truly
A Lincoln.

Ralph Waldo Emerson said that abolitionist John Brown would "make the gallows as glorious as the cross."

And Brown was a man willing to die for the sins of others—or his own. Raised in the North, he was a lifelong zealot, virulently opposed to slavery. In 1847 he told Frederick Douglass that he would free the slaves by force. Over the next decade, Brown devoted himself to violent episodes that culminated in October 1859 with a raid on the U.S. arsenal at Harpers Ferry, Virginia (left, in what is now West Virginia), apparently a step in a plan to urge a slave rebellion. He was captured and on December 2 was hanged in Charles Town. Lincoln downplayed Brown, but for many Southerners the raid was proof of a Northern plot to use force to wipe out slavery. The Civil War was beckoning.

April 14, 1861: The Stars and Bars ripples over Fort Sumter.

The seven stars in the Confederate flag represented the states that had already seceded. After decades of debate over slavery and states' rights, the North and South would settle matters the old-fashioned way—by force of arms. Fort Sumter, in the harbor of Charleston, South Carolina, was shelled for two days until the Union garrison, supplies nearly gone, surrendered on April 13. Above: The 67-year-old secessionist agitator Edmund Ruffin, who had taken part in the assault, sat for a victory photo a few days later. When the South fell, he would commit suicide.

September 17, 1862, Antietam: the bloodiest single day of the Civil War

The day dawned damply along Antietam Creek. General Robert E. Lee was driving through Maryland, looking to take the war into the North. Union General George B. McClellan, not far away and with twice as many men, finally attacked, leading to a furious clash that concluded at the graceful stone bridge above. By day's end there were 23,000 dead and wounded, equally divided between the two sides. At left, army wagons rolled after the battle; at right, Lincoln visits Antietam not long after the Union's marginal victory.

Nathan Farb

July 1–3, 1863, Gettysburg: the greatest battle ever in the Western Hemisphere

The durable legend is that Rebel General Henry Heth heard about a shoe warehouse in Gettysburg, and when his troops went to clean out the place, the battle was joined. More probably, Heth went to investigate Union movements. Unquestioned fact: Some 165,000 men met for three days of bravery and mayhem. The artillery could be heard in Pittsburgh, 140 miles away. Crippled by the shelling, with formations tangled and few reinforcements, Lee withdrew on July 4. "It is all my fault," he said as he rode along his train of wounded, which extended 14 miles. The Confederate sharpshooter below died at Devil's Den.

Hulton/Archive

"Run to Jesus—
shun the danger—
I don't expect to stay
Much longer here."

Lyrics of spirituals were often coded, and these urged slaves to board the Underground Railroad. Tradition holds that the system for sneaking slaves north ran from roughly 1830 to 1865. In fact, slaves had regularly been escaping bondage for two centuries prior. But during the mid-1800s, efforts to grease the skids certainly grew in sophistication. Harriet Tubman (above) was a Railroad engineer, helping some 300 slaves escape. In Pennsylvania, the Reverend Alexander Dobbin opened a way station in a secret room off the stairwell (left). Another stop was in Peekskill, New York (right). Coded quilts gave directions along the route. The Drunkard's pattern at left instructed, "Follow the zigzag path."

Scott Goldsmith (2)

April 9, 1865: Lacking men and matériel, Lee surrenders to Grant.

The end of the war, one might say, came as a relief. By early 1864, a Union victory was apparent, but the South fought valiantly on, inspired by the genius of Robert E. Lee, seen at right 11 days after the war at his house in Richmond. His last encampment had been down the road at left. About 620,000 soldiers had perished, including a Northern cavalryman who sought sanctuary at the Namozine Church, above, in one of the war's very last battles; his blood still stains the floorboards. This had been the first modern war, a "total war" in which the foes used all the resources they possessed. But the Union had been saved, the "fiery trial" survived. The United States was on the way to becoming a global power.

A ll persons held as slaves ... are, and henceforward shall be, free," decrees Lincoln's Emancipation Proclamation.

The verdict of the Civil War would ratify the 1863 Proclamation, and most of the newly freed people would rise out of their former quarters—such as the Florida ruins at left, a vile lodging of shell-and-lime. But where, exactly, would the liberated go? Many fled northward, but most remained in the South, often pursuing the only endeavors they had come to know. An anonymous plantation verse, of uncertain date, reads: "We raise de wheat, Dey gib us de corn, / We bake de bread, Dey gib us de cruss, / We sif de meal, Dey gib us de huss [husk]." The men below, perhaps sharecroppers, were still working King Cotton in the 1890s.

It is simply a city of mechanics, who have made the world ring with their achievements in mechanism—nothing more."

Seven thousand years ago the Agricultural Revolution saw man turn from hunter to farmer and allowed for the rise of urban civilizations in Mesopotamia, Egypt, Greece and Rome. Millennia rolled by with no equally consequential shift in the way man did business. Then, in the 18th century, the Industrial Revolution transformed river valleys in Lancashire, England, and later those of the northeastern U.S., into meccas of manufacturing. Historian Charles Cowley, looking in 1856 upon Lowell, Massachusetts (opposite), the nation's first planned industrial town, got it right with that "city of mechanics" crack. Lowell was also a city of weavers, mostly women, who operated the cotton looms; in nearby Lynn (above), women made shoes. Today in Lowell the mills house cafes and a historical park. The Industrial Revolution lives on only in the name of the city's minor-league baseball team, the Spinners.

The Industrial Revolution put many children in harm's way.

In Great Britain, Oliver Twist was the poster boy for the children of the Industrial Revolution. Charles Dickens visited Lowell, Massachusetts, during its heyday and wrote approvingly in *American Notes* of working conditions in the factories—especially as contrasted with those in his homeland. But American industry was soon emulating Britain's deplorable standards, with children as young as seven and eight being put to work. Reformers began to crusade against this new social ill, "child labor," but the disease lingered, and in the 20th century kids were still working long and dangerous hours in mines and mills (as here, in Tennessee in 1910). Congress finally passed a child-labor law in 1916, and through the years, standards have regularly been tightened to protect children.

Goodbye, God, I'm going to Bodie," a little girl is said to have uttered.

Seen today at left, Bodie was one of those towns that burned bright and short in the get-rich-quick mining frenzies of the 19th century. In its heyday—1879 to 1881—it was the "most lawless, wildest and toughest mining camp the far west has ever known." The California site is maintained in "arrested decay": The buildings are kept as they were, but there's no paved road to get there, no tourist trinkets, no McDonald's. Creede, Colorado (above), was created in the early 1890s. Richard Harding Davis wrote, "It is like a city of fresh cardboard, and the pine shanties seem to trust for support to the ... gulch in which they have squeezed themselves." This photo was taken before the business district burned down in the summer of 1892. That June, Bob Ford, the man who killed Jesse James, was shot dead in his Creede saloon by a miner named O'Kelly. Some boomtowns escaped Bodie's fate, and today Creede is still kicking.

(R) Nina Leen. (U) Woodfin Camp

Center for American Music (2)

W hat then is the American, this new man?" asked Hector St. John de Crèvecoeur in *Letters from an American Farmer* in 1782.

Having been invented politically and philosophically by the founding fathers, the American would be shaped over time by the nation's artists, writers and, indeed, inventors. A man of letters who trailblazed as an American writer was Washington Irving (opposite), who began to create the country's lore and legend in the early 19th century with his *Sketch Book,* which included both "Rip Van Winkle" and "Legend of Sleepy Hollow." (The great man is buried in New York's Sleepy Hollow Cemetery, above, once visited by the Headless Horseman.) On the 50th anniversary of the country's founding, July 4, 1826, Thomas Jefferson and John Adams both died and, in Lawrenceville, Pennsylvania, Stephen Foster (above, left) was born. His prodigious output of some 200 songs, inspired by rhythms and themes from folk songs and black spirituals, gave the country its singing voice. "Oh! Susanna" and "My Old Kentucky Home" remain part of the nation's consciousness.

I f a man does not keep pace with his companions, perhaps it is
because he hears a different drummer," wrote Henry David Thoreau.

His was a declaration for independence, arguing that, in a democracy, any odd men out are still in, and that it is allowable to live honorably poor a mile and a half from the honorably comfortable. Thoreau (opposite) published his account of life in a Walden Pond cabin in 1854; three years earlier Herman Melville (right), inspired by the fate of Captain George Pollard Jr.'s ill-starred whaleboat *Essex,* published *Moby-Dick,* in which a multiracial community of sailors sought wealth and adventure. Today in Massachusetts, Walden is much as Thoreau knew it, and the Nantucket house where Captain Pollard lived is a gift shop.

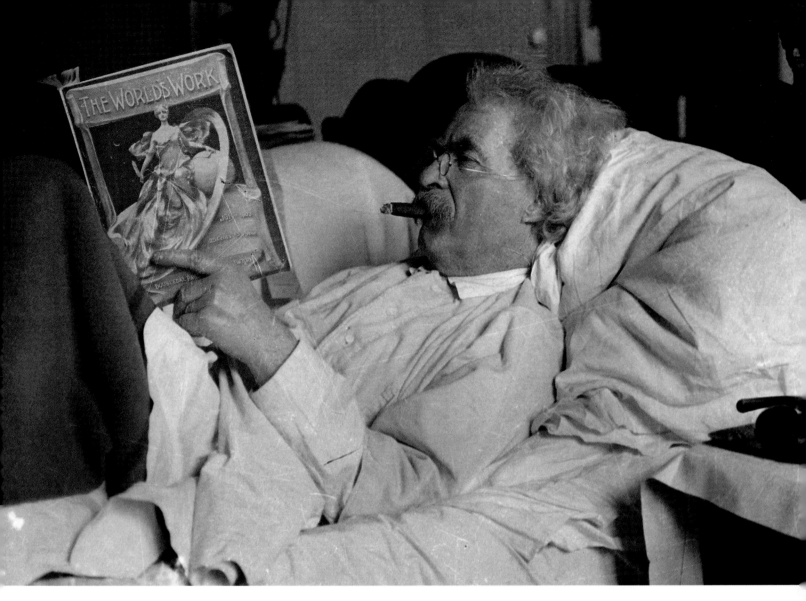

"Modern American literature comes from *Huckleberry Finn.*"

So said Ernest Hemingway of Mark Twain's masterpiece, published in 1884. The book is about freedom, as Huck and a runaway slave head down the Mississippi. "Then I thought a minute, and says to myself, hold on; s'pose you'd 'a' done right and give Jim up, would you felt better than what you do now? No, says I, I'd feel bad—" Alfred Kazin called Huck, "Odysseus in the American epic; he is all craft and good sense, and slippery as the devil." At right is Huck and Jim's island, near Twain's boyhood home in Hannibal, Missouri.

Bob Greenlee

Genius, said Thomas Edison, is "one percent inspiration and 99 percent perspiration."

It was a peculiarly American way to express it, stressing a fierce work ethic over any intrinsic brilliance. But the evidence is clear: Lightbulbs were forever going off in Edison's head. With only three months of schooling, he went on to claim 1,093 patents, which changed the way others saw and heard the world. Henry Ford, paying court to Edison in the photo at left, also altered the American way of life with his assembly-line car production. The industrialist and the inventor got the nation up and running.

F or a transitory enchanted moment man must have held his breath in the presence of this continent."

By the time F. Scott Fitzgerald wrote those words in *The Great Gatsby* (1925), man, having subdued the continent, was enchanted less with nature than with riches, speed, the future. Edith Wharton (opposite) traveled from the gilded age—of which she was a product and which she embodied, writing in bed upstairs at her Massachusetts mansion (above), letting the pages fall to the floor to be gathered by a maid—to the glittering age of 20th century America. She wrote acute psychological novels of Americans struggling against society. Fitzgerald, the modernist, was a direct literary descendant. And, alongside his troubled wife, Zelda, he too embodied the world of which he wrote.

Not in history has a modern imperial city been so completely destroyed. San Francisco is gone."

At 5:12 a.m. on April 18, 1906, a foreshock was felt throughout the Bay Area. Within a half minute a giant earthquake rent the city. Felt from southern Oregon to southern California, the quake ruptured some 270 miles of the San Andreas Fault. The epicenter was near San Francisco, where shocks severed gas mains and snapped electrical wires, starting fires throughout the city. The writer Jack London, living 40 miles from San Francisco, saw a "lurid tower" of fire that "swayed in the sky, reddening the sun, darkening the day, and filling the land with smoke." By the time he reached the city, the devastation was so thorough that London was moved to declare San Francisco "gone." It wasn't, of course, though 3,000 people were killed and 200,000 left homeless. The city rebuilt, and what's unseen today in much new construction are stabilizing systems to counter the inevitable future quakes. Older buildings remain most vulnerable. Opposite is the view from Russian Hill during the fire. Above, a similar perspective today.

In the speakeasy. Tight. I shee you, shir," wrote James Joyce in *Ulysses*.

In fact, the word "speakeasy" may go back 200 years to Irish *spake-aisy* shops. In the 1880s, an Irish woman in Pittsburgh who sold liquor without a license admonished her clients to "spake aisy." Whatever the origin, after Prohibition began in 1920, a "speak" was an illegal place where the activities were bibulous and on the q.t. (left, in New York City in 1933). It could be crude or elegant. At many, if you weren't known, you hoped that "Joe sent me" would get you past the peephole. By the end of the '20s the country had more speakeasies than it ever had saloons, and though bootleg booze was often dangerous, millions drank it. In 1933, Prohibition was repealed, and liquor was legit again. Many former speaks went on to respectability, including New York's '21' (above), where a two-ton false-front door that once hid the wine cellar now opens wide.

Chris Johns/National Geographic

Hulton Archive

Some people tell us that there ain't no Hell, But they never farmed, so how can they tell?"

Nobody knows who came up with that rhyme in 1940, but it was a soul who had seen his share of crops. Or the lack of them. In the early 1930s a severe drought set in across much of the country, and nowhere was harder hit than the southern Great Plains—Kansas, Oklahoma, New Mexico, Texas, Colorado (right, in 1939, just before the rains would finally return). It was already tough times, what with the Depression, but then the winds kicked up and drove across the barren, bone-dry fields, rising into "black blizzards" that reached five miles high. One underlying problem in the region was that a lot of the natural grassland, which served as a wind break, had been plowed up or overgrazed. When the storms came in the spring, which they usually did, the new crops weren't able to hold the soil. Animals and people lost their way, maybe had their lungs torn up. A single storm in March 1935 wrecked half the wheat crop in Kansas, a quarter of it in Oklahoma, all of it in Nebraska. The amount of soil lost to erosion was stunning: One storm carried 350 million tons of dirt to the East Coast. The people left, too, more than half of them. But some stayed, toughed it out, like the Fischers of Oklahoma, above, who in 1984 represented four generations of a family that had survived the Dust Bowl. By enduring, the Fischers avoided the fate of those so sadly limned in Steinbeck's *The Grapes of Wrath*. Since the '30s, much has been learned, but slipshod agriculture still destroys crops and lives on the Great Plains.

Peter Essick/Aurora

God never intended Southern California to be anything but desert."

So wrote the historian Carey McWilliams in 1946, adding, "Man has made it what it is." The paucity of water resources has been a nagging concern since the pueblo days of Los Angeles. Any development in the region ultimately turns on the availability of water. In 1941, the city began to divert four of the five major Sierran streams that feed Mono Lake. Without that influx, Mono—one of the oldest lakes in North America—dropped by 45 vertical feet and doubled in salinity to three times that of seawater. Consequently, this major breeding ground for waterfowl has undergone a 98 percent decline in usage. But there is room for guarded optimism. In the past 25 years, Mono has become a cause célèbre; bicyclists lugged water the 320 miles from L.A. in protest. In 1994, legal levels of diversion were fixed, and so far the water has risen nine feet, with yet another nine feet to come. The otherworldly limestone structures at right are called tufa towers. Before L.A. intervened in 1941, they were all under water.

Carr Clifton/Minden Pictures

Our own oil ... was catching fire slowly and was incinerating toward us."

James Cory, who was a Pfc. on the doomed *Arizona,* recalled December 7, 1941, like it was yesterday. So, too, would every American who heard the news that day, over the radio or from a neighbor across the back fence. The surprise Japanese attack on Pearl Harbor was terrible but in the end provided a rallying cry that helped America band together to defeat a brutal Axis enemy. The black smoke billowing above is mainly from the *Arizona;* the chaplain's clock from the battleship reflects forever a heartbreaking moment. Of the 2,403 Americans killed that morning, nearly half went down with the *Arizona.* Their memorial (opposite) was dedicated in 1962.

Herd 'em up, pack 'em off and give 'em the inside room in the badlands ... That goes for all of them."

That was the opinion of columnist Henry McLemore and millions of other Americans regarding people of Japanese heritage living in the U.S. at the time of the Pearl Harbor bombing. This thinking carried the day, and not long after the December 7, 1941, attack, Santa Anita in southern California was converted from a racetrack to one of 16 "assembly centers." Eventually some 120,000 West Coast Japanese-Americans, citizens and resident aliens alike, were relocated to internment camps under the presumption that those nearest the Pacific would be of most use to Japan as spies. In 1944 the last of them was freed, and the government has since made financial reparations to survivors. At Santa Anita today, the concern is with win, place and show.

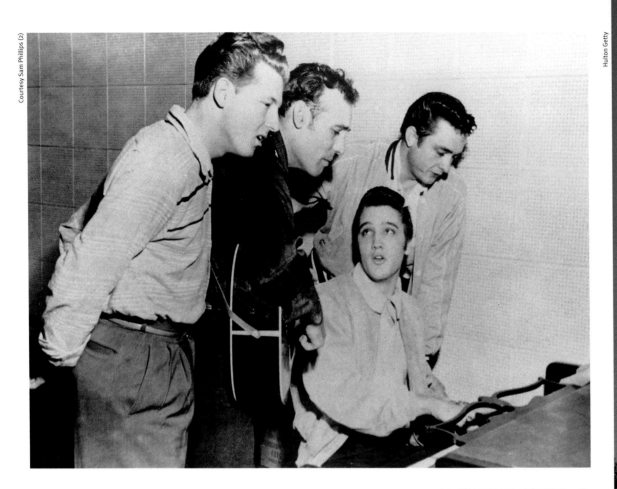

I was shooting for that damn row that hadn't been plowed."

Sam Phillips had wanted to be a criminal defense lawyer, to help the disadvantaged. But in 1950 he ended up opening the Memphis Recording Service, cutting discs mainly with arcane black artists. Two years later he started Sun Records, and his reputation for painstakingness attracted the attention of some amazing local talent (above, Jerry Lee Lewis, Carl Perkins, Elvis Presley and Johnny Cash). Elvis, of course, was the real deal, the white boy who sounded black that Phillips had sought. But Sun had money woes, and in 1955 Elvis was sold to RCA, for just $35,000.

Bernard Hoffman

Margaret Bourke-White

As long ago as the 1st century B.C., Cicero made reference to the *"suburbani"* outside Rome.

It is doubtful, however, whether the Roman version resembled the suburb called Levittown. In 1947, Levitt & Sons began to build low-cost housing for veterans back from the war. The last of their 17,447 single-unit homes was completed four years later. While the 1950s may have been a time of rigid conformity—that's 1950 in Levittown, New York, above, and 1957 over Levittown, Pennsylvania, right—the recent epoch of individualism has inspired the grand sort of renovation wrought by Maureen Hare on her New York Levitt, below.

Ed Bailey/AP

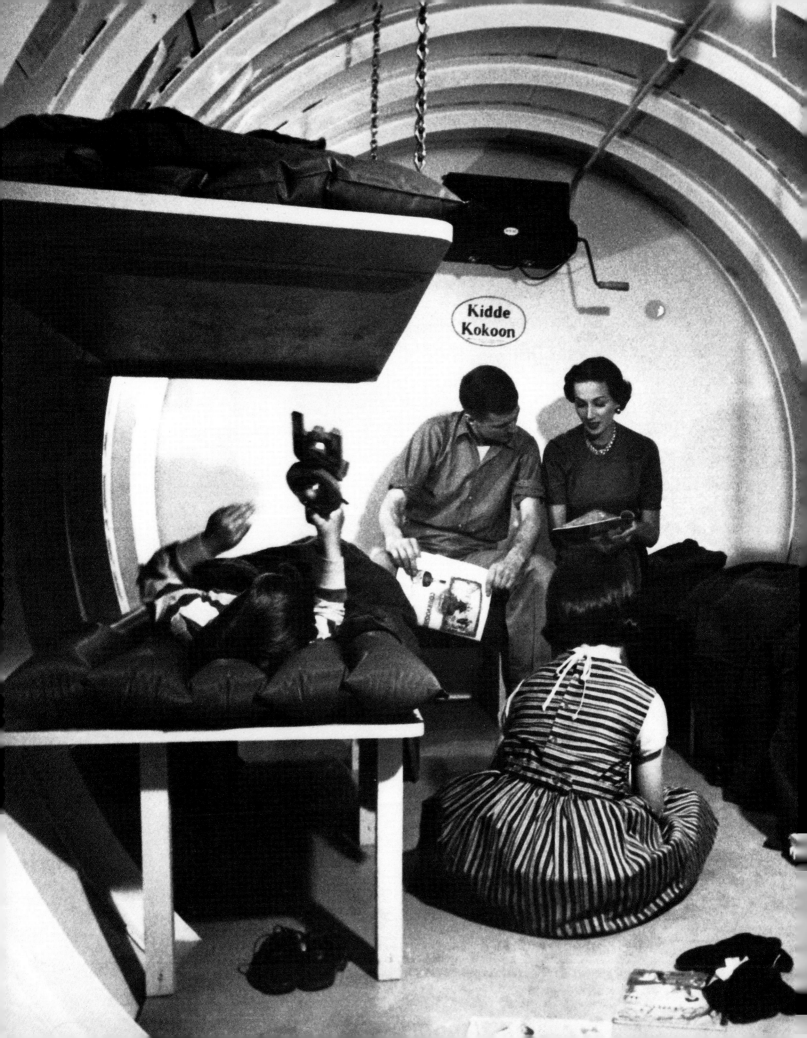

W e are developing improved warning systems which will make it possible to sound [a] warning on buzzers right in your homes ... "

President John F. Kennedy wrote those words in a "message" to Americans that appeared in LIFE on September 15, 1961. The letter, and the accompanying article, "How You Can Survive Fallout," jolted a nation already jittery from the cold war. In underlining the need for precautions, the article resorted to mathematics: "About five million people, less than 3% of the population, would die. This in itself is a ghastly number. But you have to look at it coldly. Unprepared, there is one chance in four that you and your family will die. Prepared, you and your family could have 97 chances out of 100 to survive." It was a time of living daily with death.

Fallout shelters first took root in the United States in 1949 when President Harry S. Truman revealed that the Soviets had the A-bomb, but the growth spurt came a decade later as "sputnik" and "U2" became all-too-ordinary terms. (The American nuclear unit at left was photographed in their Garden City, New York, shelter in 1955.) Today, many of the dugouts remain, but they are just as likely to serve as wine cellars.

From a sixth floor window a gunner shot him down, He was in Dallas town."

In 1965, when the Byrds sang "He Was a Friend of Mine," their lament for John F. Kennedy, the national wound was still raw, hurting. Of course, the healing process had been severely retarded by the fact that the assassination, and its aftermath, was shrouded in mystery. Who were these people, were they conspirators, why in God's name had they done this? On November 22, 1963, the photographers and bystanders below were captured some 30 seconds after the shooting. In the right rear is the Texas School Book Depository, where sniper Lee Harvey Oswald had set up shop. Taken from a similar perspective, the recent photograph at left shows an X that was placed on Elm Street by local Kennedy-assassination researchers. It marks the spot where the fatal shot hit home.

Think of all the hate there is in Red China! Then take a look around to Selma, Alabama!"

These words from Barry McGuire's 1965 hit, "Eve of Destruction," reflected the unrest in America. Racial strife had been percolating since school segregation was banned in 1954. There followed the Montgomery bus boycott, the sit-in campaign at a Greensboro lunch counter, Freedom Rides. In many southern states, blacks couldn't vote; to address this the Rev. Martin Luther King Jr. organized a march from Selma to the state capital. Then King had to go to Washington, but the folks in Selma set out anyway, on March 7. When they reached the Edmund Pettus Bridge (reflected in the window above), a posse of state troopers armed with tear gas and billy clubs drove them to a housing project and beat them cruelly. "Bloody Sunday" drew national attention, paving the way to the Voting Rights Act of 1965.

By the time we got to Woodstock, We were half a million strong, And everywhere there was song and celebration."

They came to a field of dreams, a psychedelic pasture ceded by one Max Yasgur, a farmer in Bethel—not Woodstock—New York, to a generation that bought into peace, music and love in an era of social schism. And despite obstacles—staging snafus, gremlins in the sound system, and rain, rain, rain—it was one for the ages. But 1969 would be both crescendo and coda to the dream; the violence-shrouded Altamont concert was just four months away. Today, Woodstock lives on as the incessant marketing of an ideal. Young people gathered again in '94 (right) and at later "Woodstocks," but these were simply ways to sell expensive water.

Nathan Farb

Johnstown Flood Museum

The sound sweeping down toward Johnstown was "a roar like thunder."

On May 31, 1889, a dam burst and a wall of water as high as 40 feet washed over the Pennsylvania town that had been built on a floodplain at the fork of two rivers (above and left), killing 2,209. In the summer of 1993, rainfalls of more than a foot in the Midwest caused fantastic flooding, including here in Mississippi (opposite). A century between, yet similar causes: Building where floods will come. And failed, futile attempts to harness nature.

Acid rain in one New England storm had a pH of 2.4, which exceeds the acidity of vinegar.

Scientists call it acid deposition, but the common term is acid rain: any precipitation with abnormal levels of sulfuric or nitric acids. Auto exhaust and the industrial burning of coal and oil are the primary culprits, although volcanoes and forest fires can also contribute. The harshest results are seen in eastern Canada, the eastern U.S. and western Europe, which are all downwind of heavy industrial regions.

Acid rain affects water, forests (above, in North Carolina), soil and buildings, and can worsen health problems. Even things like cars may be damaged: In one summer storm, rain leached away the yellow from a lime-green car, leaving blue raindrop-shaped spots. In the 1990s governments mandated emissions controls, and the rain is becoming less acid, but the issue is still up in the air.

On radar, this bird looks as big as a ⅛" ball bearing.

It is an F-117A stealth fighter. Prior to its unveiling in 1988—and a dramatic performance in 1991's Operation Desert Storm—the plane had been buried in extremely hush-hush research and development. The genesis of the Nighthawk, as it would be dubbed, dates back to a top secret 1975 Pentagon briefing on Soviet advances in weapons and electronics. In the 1973 Yom Kippur War, Israel had lost 109 planes in 18 days, and a disturbing study revealed that in a Soviet-American clash, using similar planes, training and ground defenses, the U.S. Air Force would be destroyed in just 17 days. A Lockheed executive was at that conference, and the firm's "Skunk Works" operation in Burbank, California, looked for solutions. The resultant aircraft of flat, angular surfaces coated with a secret radar-absorbent material was impervious to detection. Its computer program was so advanced that the Air Force bought the system for all its attack planes. Despite blistering ground fire during Desert Storm, the Nighthawk owned the skies.

Vanishing **America**

Vanishing America

Consider the boreal forest: Giant trees forming a thick canopy, covering much of the continent. Long after American Indians had spread across the land, the woods remained essentially unaltered. Some have said, not trying to be fanciful, that a squirrel could have gone branch-to-branch from the Atlantic to the Mississippi. This forest, one of the planet's largest, defined this place—a place that looked, to the first Europeans, wild, untamed, ripe.

In 1633, one William Wood recorded his vision of the New World for the edification of those back home in England. "The timber of the country grows straight and tall, some trees being twenty, some thirty foot high, before they spread forth their branches," he wrote. Of animals, he reported alewives "in such multitudes as is almost incredible, pressing up such shallow waters as will scarce permit them to swim" and birds so plentiful as to be nothing but sitting ducks: "If I should tell you how some have killed a hundred geese in a week, fifty ducks at a shot, forty teals at another, it may be counted impossible though nothing more certain." As Wood dutifully reported, the English were already at work, changing things.

Barely more than two centuries later, on January 24, 1855, Henry David Thoreau, assessing the same neck of the woods described earlier by Wood, rued that so much had been altered. Whither the two-inch-round strawberries described by Wood? To find giant forests, one needed to travel north and visit "the sample still left in Maine." Hunters had continued their energetic assault: "Eagles are probably less common; pigeons, of course ... heath cocks all gone ... and turkeys ... Probably more owls then, and cormorants, etc. etc., sea-fowl generally." Others than Thoreau called it progress, and it would only accelerate.

Today approximately three percent of America's primeval forest remains, and this serves as metaphor for all else that has changed—or vanished. Scores of bird and animal species have disappeared from the earth in the past 200 years. In America, hunters killed off the last Eastern bison in 1825, the last Eastern elk in 1855. Millions of passenger pigeons used to live in the forest east of the Great Plains. The last one died in 1914 in a zoo. The Indians who had been well known to Wood and familiar to Thoreau were, over time, plagued by introduced illnesses, hunted down, incarcerated, pushed about, assimilated. Their ancient culture was altered, large pieces of it lost, forgotten or forsaken.

Landscape was overrun or filled in, and the same could be said of many American traditions. As the melting pot bubbled and boiled, fresh urban and suburban trends continuously made the old obsolete. The last cowboy headed home from the range, and sandlot baseball gave way to skateboards. Some—not Thoreauvians—called it progress.

The iconic photograph on the preceding pages depicts a group of Navajos making their way through Arizona's Canyon de Chelly. The picture was taken circa 1920 by Edward Curtis, who in the early 20th century published 40 volumes of photos of American Indians. The beguiling family at right are Pawnees. The man wears a peace medal, probably a family heirloom that had been bestowed by the government at a treaty signing. The Pawnees' trappings and the Navajos' horses have, through the years, been usurped by Levi's and Chevys.

Oh, give me a home, where the buffalo roam ... "

These words and the simple, lilting melody from "Home on the Range" well evoke the American cowboy, one of the country's indelible symbols. Of course, there are still brave men on horseback who work cattle, but whenever possible they let machines or helicopters do the job. The heyday of the cowboy—a small man (so as not to tire the horse), usually of Anglo-American, Spanish-Mexican-Indian, or African-American stock—ran from the end of the Civil War to the mid-1880s. After that, fences and railroads would seal the fate of the trail drive (right, near the end in Wyoming), which now exists solely for dudes willing to pay for a macho getaway.

Oklahoma Dugout.

W oodman,
spare that tree!
Touch not a
single bough!"

Sentiments such as those voiced by George P. Morris were slow to cut into America's consciousness. Eventually, however, the loss of grand trees did become an issue. In 1892 photographer Darius Kinsey went to the camps of the Pacific Northwest to document the takedown of massive cedars and redwoods. Elsewhere in America, at precisely the same time, there were no trees, and prairie families like the Oklahomans above lived in sod houses. While science informs tree farming today, battles continue over remnant old-growth forest. As for the rugged lifestyles: Loggers live at home, not in camps. And the idea of making a house out of "Nebraska marble" slabs held together by roots seems medieval.

Darius Kinsey/Culver Pictures. Inset: Western History Collections/University of Oklahoma

Build me straight, O worthy master! Stanch and strong, a goodly vessel."

Longfellow was, of course, really talking about the Ship of State in his 1849 poem *The Building of the Ship*. It was an apt metaphor, as the sea and shipping played a decisive role in the rise to power of the United States. This picture of a dock on New York City's South Street was taken circa 1886 by Alice Austen. Born in 1866, she found her calling at the age of 10 when she was given a dry-plate camera from Europe by her uncle. Austen specialized in the world around her, and much of her work contains images of New York Harbor, which faced the mansion where she grew up. Today, the nature of shipping has changed dramatically, as has the South Street Seaport. In the manner of other once-decrepit waterfronts around the country, it is now a magnet for museum-goers, mart-hounds and mimes.

Polly, put the kettle on, And let's drink tea."

These cheery words from the Mother Goose nursery rhyme surely capture the spirit of this 1905 women's enclave in Black River Falls, Wisconsin—and countless other communities across the land. These ladies met regularly at one another's house for tea, sewing and a lively examination of local happenings. The photographer was Charles Van Schaick, whose wife, Ida (standing), served as hostess for the occasion. At the time, rich women essentially lived on pedestals, while poor ones knew no end to the workday. The middle class, as Oliver Jensen wrote in the lovely volume *American Album,* was "hedged about by a propriety even more restrictive than their formidable undergarments." At this springtime get-together (which they called a Kensington), the rugs provided both a windbreak and privacy. The amenities included tea, lemonade and cookies. Such a gathering today would perhaps include wine along with Chinese or Mexican takeout. And, oh, yes, men as well, since women and men no longer live in two different worlds.

Not long ago, the West was free, open, there for the taking.

For the longest time, the western terminus of the country was widely considered to be St. Louis. Beyond that was the expanse, a place to strike it rich, where they were positively giving land away. That frontier image lingered well into the 20th century; big-league baseball wasn't even played left of the Mississippi until 1957. This photo was taken in the late 1800s in California. It shows the sale of 2,500 lots on Ocean Beach. Today that milelong stretch of San Diego lies amid tony resort towns like La Jolla and Del Mar and is a stone's throw from the Padres' ballpark.

"Water is a very good servant, but it is a cruel master."

John Bullein wrote these words in 1562, but they are true for all time. In the early 20th century, Butler, Tennessee (top, in 1902), was a quiet place where a turkey drive was big news. But at times, there was real drama: floods. Every few years a nearby river overflowed,

Ulysses Miller

Christopher Green

drowning people and ruining crops. Then in 1941 the government approved the construction of a dam and—just where Butler lay—a reservoir (above, in 1999). Butler would have disappeared, had many of its residents not taken action. Granted, it was eerie to see homes lifted by hydraulic jack and shunted two and a half miles away, but it meant the town would survive. Today, with a population of 1,200, life is good, save for one thing. "We'll never be able to show our grandchildren where we came from, except in pictures."

"Animals hear about death for the first time when they die."

The philosopher Schopenhauer was referring to animals' living for the present. But humans, who study animals—and often decide their fate—can see the writing on the wall. Owing to habitat loss, there are some 50 Florida panthers left, and only half their terrain is held publicly, not a good omen in the growing Sunshine State. There hasn't been a verified sighting of the ivory-billed woodpecker, the Holy Grail for birders, in the U.S. since 1972. Their diet and the vast felling of timber just didn't jibe.

James Balog/Tony Stone. Inset: A.A. Allen/Cornell University

At bottom, the desert tortoise and the bull trout are listed as threatened. The tortoise has been a case study in litigation for years, and among its woes are illegal collection and vandalism by humans and the loss of forage plants to grazing livestock. Found mainly in the Northwest, bull trout need clear, cold water and are going under to logging and road building. The black-footed ferret (top left), long considered America's most endangered mammal, was even thought extinct until 1981. Captive animals were then bred and released into the wild, and the creature now stands a fighting chance. The world-famous Kirtland's warbler nests only in tiny, dense stands of young jack pines in a small area of Michigan. The endangered warbler's nests are heavily parasitized by cowbirds.

William H. Mullins/Photo Researchers

Todd Haiman

Culver Pictures

W hoever wants to know the heart and mind of America had better learn baseball ... "

The French-born historian Jacques Barzun made that observation in 1954, and it is true today. In fact, more people than ever watch Major League baseball. But the Grand Old Game is quite different at ground zero. It used to be that children and baseball went hand in glove. If you took a stroll, you wouldn't have far to go before coming across kids in a pickup game. They didn't need fancy gear: The ball was likely taped together and a sweater served as second base. Today, there's a game only if it has been organized by (often rabid) adults. Where did the innocence go? Was it Vietnam? Watergate? The erosion of family? The 'net? It's difficult to say.

American Images

Sometimes a picture tells the whole truth and nothing but the truth. At other times, a picture deceives. It barely hints at a story. The closer we look, the more mysterious the image becomes. What seems to be a Dalí painting—an eerily dripping piece of surrealism—turns out to be the most natural, elemental thing imaginable. Sometimes a rock is not a rock but, rather, a ball. And that face: Is it America's most famous woman or ... Elvis?

In revealing the America that lies beneath the surface and behind the scenes, it is interesting—and often fun—to look at a final few images that don't reveal all they know.

National Archives

Michael Rougier

Ancient China?

On June 17, 1972, security guard Frank Wills noticed some tape over a door lock, called the police and foiled a break-in by five burglars. Two long years later, a mesmerized nation looked on as a President resigned in disgrace. This is the Watergate hotel in Washington, D.C.

Fred Hirschmann

A.Y. Owen

Southern Living

Wedding Cake, by Salvador Dalí?

Fashioned over thousands of years and found in a realm of silence and darkness, these lacelike things may be measured in inches or hundreds of feet. They are created when calcite-rich groundwater trickles down a wall. As it descends, it layers into shapes like these extraordinary offerings, which are found at Blanchard Springs Caverns in Mountain View, Arkansas. They are neither stalactite nor stalagmite. They are flowstone.

From the Collection of Mick Jagger and Keith Richards?

A playa is desert that sometimes becomes a lake. That big stone at left, in California's Death Valley, has been taken for a ride. Maybe an earthquake set it in motion, but more likely wind caused it to aquaplane. The stone disk at right was found at Georgia's Etowah Indian Mounds. In a thousand-year-old game called chunkey, Creek ancestors rolled it and hurled poles to where they thought it would stop. Gambling was rife.

Actually, Only One Lantern Was Needed ...

... for the British were coming by land to arrest John Hancock and Samuel Adams. Longfellow did get it right: The signal to be shone from Boston's Old North Church was "one [lamp] if by land, two if by sea." But he was wrong that Paul Revere did the signaling. Revere was in Charlestown, ready to ride and warn his fellow patriots as soon as he received the word—which he did at 10 p.m. on April 18, 1775.

The Holy Scroll of a Whole Subculture

Some things it wasn't: Written in a Benzedrine-and-coffee-fueled rush. (The author later said caffeine was the sole drug.) Written on a single roll of paper. (The author taped the pages together subsequently.) Partially eaten by a dog. (The last pages were simply lost.) What it was and is: The original manuscript of the Beat Generation classic, Jack Kerouac's *On the Road*. It was sold at auction in 2001 for $2.46 million.

War of the Worlds?

They're loud, metallic and at least 100 feet high. One in Hawaii looms 20 stories tall and is wider than a football field. Their power derives from solar energy in concert with the irregularities of the earth's surface. They are windmills, specifically wind turbines (here, a wind farm two hours north of Los Angeles). The Department of Energy hopes they will provide five percent of the nation's electricity by 2020.

A Shell Game

One of the last unspoiled Atlantic coastal wetlands lies in the 46,000-acre Timucuan Ecological and Historic Preserve in Jacksonville, Florida. In the picture at right, an overturned tree exposed this large gathering of shells. But this isn't simply a residue from tides long since departed. Rather, it is an oyster shell midden, the remains of an Indian feast that may date back 1,000 years.

Is This the King or America's Queen?

This hunka hunka copper sculpture is not, in fact, a rendering of the king of rock 'n' roll, Elvis Presley, but of one Auguste-Charlotte Bartholdi, mother of the French sculptor Frédéric-Auguste Bartholdi. She's big: Her nose is 4 ½ feet long and each eye is 2 ½ feet across. And she's famous: As *Liberty Enlightening the World* (a.k.a. the Statue of Liberty) she has graced New York Harbor since arriving there, a gift from the citizens of France, in 1884.